GERALDINE MOORKENS BYRNE

Dreams of Reality

A Collection of Poetry

First published by PPP Publishing 2024

Copyright © 2024 by Geraldine Moorkens Byrne

All rights reserved. No part of this publication may be reproduced, stored or transmitted in any form or by any means, electronic, mechanical, photocopying, recording, scanning, or otherwise without written permission from the publisher. It is illegal to copy this book, post it to a website, or distribute it by any other means without permission.

Geraldine Moorkens Byrne asserts the moral right to be identified as the author of this work.

Geraldine Moorkens Byrne has no responsibility for the persistence or accuracy of URLs for external or third-party Internet Websites referred to in this publication and does not guarantee that any content on such Websites is, or will remain, accurate or appropriate.

These poems are entirely a work of fiction. The names, characters and incidents portrayed in it are the work of the author's imagination. Any resemblance to actual persons, living or dead, events or localities is entirely coincidental

First edition

ISBN: 978-1-7396496-5-4

This book was professionally typeset on Reedsy. Find out more at reedsy.com

To Mark, with thanks to Aengus Óg

Contents

Foreword   v
Preface   x
Acknowledgments   xii

I   Dreams of Reality: In the Grove

Encounter	3
Cliona by the Shore	4
Death of the Hero	6
Lament for Setanta	8
Crossings	9
Meeting Bríd By Water	10
Imbolg	11
Bean Chrosach	12
Yule at the court of Maeve	13
Breaking Faith With Aengus Óg	15
Apologies to Aengus Óg	17
Bealtaine	19
Lughnasadh	22
Solstice	23
Down by Ben Bulben	27
Snow in Dublin	28
Swans and Chimney Stacks	30
Dowsing	31
Hidden Jester	33
The Jester	35

Ancestor	36
Lower me not	38
Requiem	40
Night Chorus	43
Territory	45

II   Dreams of Reality: At the Gate

Eriu Addresses the False Kings	49
Aisling	51
Where Once Stood Tribes	53
The Host of the Morrigan Marches Again	55
Aylan	57
The Economics of Power	59
The Madness of Women	60
What Shall You Teach Your Son?	62
Ar Scáth a Chéile	65
The Dublin Rosc	66
Sparks	68
Edda's Poem	70
Pussy Riots or Ailurophobia in Russian Life	72
Another Angry Black Woman Speaks	74
See Me	77
This Poem Has No Planning Permission	79
Vote Early and Often	80

III   Dreams of Reality: By the Fireside

At Work, My Grandfather	85
Pilgrimage	88
Irish Cowboys	90
What I gave up for New Year	92
Send Up A Flare, My Lovelies	95

Saving Sylvie	96
Secrets of The Dead	98
Making Amends	100
The Old Familiar Faces	102
Make up your mind	103
Making Links	105
Stolen	107
On stony ground, You fall like rain	108
By Your Presence Are You Known.	109
Late Coffee	111
For my husband, Poems that are not Valentines	113
Love letters from a Busy Life	116
The committee for the Formation of Pagan Creation theories	118
Transparent Years	121
Ladies Day	122
Sit Here	123
The Last Word	125

IV   Dreams of Reality: In your mind

The Alzheimer Series	129
Questions	131
Preservation	132
You Have to Laugh	133
Red Tape	134
Side Effects	136
Positivity	137
Nights Out	138
Manifesto	139
After	141
The First Year Without You	142
In Absentia	143

About the Author	144
Also by Geraldine Moorkens Byrne	146

Foreword

Dreams of Reality

*"We dwell by the shore now
  And bless the white thimble,
  the rue grows around us
  like weeds on a grave..."*
  from "Cliona by the Shore"

I am honoured to be asked to write the foreword to this book of profound and often beautiful poetry (often, because sometimes beauty has to take the backseat).

I am the founder of Daughters of the Flame, an interfaith, mostly Pagan, Brigidine flame-tending group which lit its first candle on Imbolc 1993. I am also the author of A Brigit of Ireland Devotional – Sun Among Stars, a compendium of poetry, prayers, and essays for those wishing to deepen their understanding of Brigit, goddess and saint, and I publish a blog of Brigit poetry, Stone on the Belly, on which Geraldine's poetry has appeared.

Geraldine Moorkens Byrne is a woman of conscience, passion, and art. I met her first on social media; with her in Ireland and me in Canada, the only way we could have met. I was attracted to her initially because of her interests: besides poetry, the history, folklore, politics, mythology, music, and people of Ireland, seen by her not in a dry or distant way, but as vital, worthy, and alive. As I grew to know her I appreciated equally her obvious values: the importance of living with awareness, hospitality, justice, and compassion, to name a few. I began to read her books, beginning with her novel, The Body Politic, in 2021, and was impressed with her skill, her dynamic and very Irish humour popping up in the midst of a serious tale, and her intimate knowledge of the workings of politics and public relations in 2020s Dublin. (Not to mention her having written a darn good mystery.) I have read everything of hers I could get my hands on, ever since.

This woman laughs a lot. She is fiercely loving toward her family and her people. She has a deep expertise in her areas of interest and, as writer, teacher, or friend, shares that expertise willingly, with clarity and inspiration. Her writing is vividly informed by her experience of life as a woman, a specifically Irish woman, whose family's rich history is keenly felt. And Geraldine does not just write about life, she writes for life. Her poems have been used in theatre, in funerals, in protests, in divorce, in rituals of love. She writes for what she stands for, and she stands up, like many great women before her, for those who are mistreated both individually and as a class.

She has a powerful voice and she is not afraid to share it.

As Geraldine's website states, "Her poetry draws on a variety of inspirational sources - Old Irish mythology, Irish literary forms, modern politics mixed with the ancient tradition of Satire."

The subtitles of the sections of Dreams of Reality alert us to its three main themes: spirit, politics, and community. Within them, we encounter deities and heroes, outrage and tenderness, an outward gaze at the world around her, and an inward gaze as she ponders those she loves. Geraldine's deep respect, her reverence, for the land she dwells on is recognizable in these poems. Her love for and sense of responsibility to that land and to the people, spirits, and deities of Ireland is evident, beginning with the first poem, "Death of the Hero." Told in a cadence that evokes the myths themselves, grief over the death of Cú Chulainn is movingly announced to all affected, friend and foe. Her perspectives are intimate, surprising, drawing the reader into the gristle of a tale, not simply glancing at its surface. A moment's encounter with a wild stag somehow captures an entire landscape, a handful of words from a fortune teller aligns us against her decrier.

> "The crows
>   startle black against
>   the spread of the year's last finery
>   a mantle of splendour
>   as the sun crowns the day."
>   from "Down by Ben Bulben"

Geraldine leads us from this world to the Other; willingly, with her, we throw our fortune in with Maeve of the Sidhe, Warrior Queen. Her Sidhe are not the floating fairies of Victorian England. They are vivid and unpredictable, with heft and gravitas. In her hands, we move in and out of this and the Otherworld, with ease "swinging out over chasms of infinity" where they overlap. We could not ask for a more trustworthy guide into their world then Geraldine. And when the poet breaks off with Angus Óg, god of love, our hearts break with hers. Her later apology to him is equally affecting. Her Rosc, "Eriu Addresses The False Kings Of Ireland," confronts proponents of rape culture, self-proclaimed "kings," putting into the hands of their opponents a powerful charge:

> *"Your ramparts fall before the anger of the Druids*
>   *And the Wise Women will make bread from the fire*
>   *Of your roof,*
>   *The earth rises against you*
>   *The stones and bones and blood of the land*
>   *Reject you and your band"*
>   from "Eriu Addresses The False Kings Of Ireland"

Geraldine looks deeply and widely at the world around her. There is nothing beyond her caring, nothing beyond her ken. Finding humour and hope at the ending of the Celtic Tiger, she has a frank discussion with Éire, well dressed in green, with her Hermés handbag. She reveals a wart or two in her frustrated poem about trying to learn to dowse. A darker humour emerges in "Requiem:" "an emotional response to the attitudes of Nuns and Priests to us as young women."

Geraldine's passion as she speaks out for the wronged is a shout from the hilltops themselves. Humour gone, her reaction to the response of Ireland and the EU to the migrant crisis is painfully summarized in her poem, "Aylan." She sees in the young Syrian boy, washed up on a Turkish beach, her own son, who thrives today despite the treatment of poor Irish like her family during the Great Hunger. "The Dublin Rosc" rails against the racist, far right riots of 2023. Her honesty and sensitivity when she writes of her grandfather, and her father in his elder years, as caretaker and loving but exhausted daughter, are straightforward and compelling. Anyone who has every done vigil at a loved one's deathbed will be moved by "Manifesto," from the brilliant "The Alzheimer Series" in the final section of the book.

I am deeply grateful to have Geraldine in my life, as a friend, as a writer whose words I eagerly consume, as someone to look to for wisdom and truthfulness. I urge you to welcome her visionings into your reader's heart today. Savour her words, whether they move you to joy or rouse you to fight. Sit with her innate intelligence, let her show you your world as she perceives it. Let her poems take up residence in you, "like the solid, recurring bass note of a drum / beating like a heart." We are blessed to have them.

"I saw my Grandfather at work,
   bent. He was old by then
   and white haired, my father
   dark and upright.
   I watched the old man
   handle wood like it was
   his lover; all his tenderness
   and poetry in the making"
   from "At Work, My Grandfather"

Mael Brigde
   Vancouver, Canada

Mael Brigde is a highly regarded writer and teacher from Canada with a deep and sincere connection to Ireland. She is the author of *A Brigit of Ireland Devotional-Sun among Stars* (Moon Books 2021) as well as beautiful works of speculative fiction (writing as Casey June Wolf) including her collection *Finding Creatures & Other Stories (2008)* and many published short stories and poetry. She runs online courses dedicated to Brigit, details of which can be found here https://linktr.ee/maelbrigde#

She is the founder of the Brigidine *Daughters of the Flame.*

Preface

A lot has happened in the 8 years since I first (roughly) published this collection, in e-book form only, back in 2016. A paperback version was always intended but life, novel writing, retirement, Covid, a bereavement and more, all intervened. In a way, I'm glad they did. This is a better collection for the wait.

Not only does it now contain more poems, published in various media over the intervening years but it contains Bedside Manners, the Alzheimer's poem collection written to highlight the plight of family carers in Ireland (and elsewhere.) This is dedicated to the memory of my dad, Charles Byrne. I also got to spend a lot of time considering what poems to include. There are some that were published and indeed, were considered successful that I have omitted and some that I may be the only one who loves, that I have included. Each one is here for a reason, and what at first glance may seem random, actually reflects an evolution in belief, understanding and interests during my life.

And some I just like the sound of, and that's okay too.

I hope you enjoy this collection. Some poems are ideal for ceremonies, and have been used for such while some others have been performed in theatre. If you wish to use any of the poems, please contact me. You'll find all the details in the back of the book. I usually say yes, unless you're planning something nefarious (and even then, it's a maybe.) I owe most of my imagination to a lifetime of reading, to parents who encouraged without hot housing, and to access to books of all types from a very early age. Ireland, our mythology and heritage, our magic and spirituality, form the bedrock of my work.

I am always open to feedback and to conversations about my work.

Geraldine Moorkens Byrne

PPP Publishing started life as the Pagan Poetry Pages in the early days of the internet, and evolved into a poetry collective that to date has published four volumes of poetry, several mystery books and one children's book. It is an entirely voluntary and haphazard organization, and any typos, errors or flaws should be embraced as proof that gloriously fallible humans created this book rather than AI.

Acknowledgments

Thanks are owed to Mael Brigde (Casey June Wolf) for her kind encouragement and for writing the foreword, a task she undertook with grace and great forbearance for my disorganization; and to the poets of the PPP, including Gina Bass, Maureen Aisling Duffy-Boose, Simone L Hogan and Kevin V Moore.

Personal thanks are very much owed to my family, especially my husband Mark who attends poetry readings without complaint and my mother Maria Moorkens Byrne, who reads everything I write. Over the years I have received validation and advice from many other poets, and from editors and publishers, all of whom make the community of poets a wonderful place. I am singularly blessed in cousins, who are the kindest cheerleaders imaginable. My heart, as ever, is with my two boys, my Oak and my Raven, who make this world worth fighting for.

I

Dreams of Reality: In the Grove

Poems of Spirit

Encounter

Light and dark at play
  cross the dappled water
  I hear the frost break
  underfoot, like glass

Horned and hooved, pawing
  at the frozen ground, antlered.
  Lowering crown, challenging-
  playfully, I think. A forest Pan.
  Breath suspended in tendrils on
  icy air; we stare transfixed.

Reluctantly, you turn from me,
  relinquish me to the gathering dusk.
  Darkened skies pass across the plains
  and rain turns to snow in the forests.
  All trace gone except in my mind's eye
  and the grand look of your own.

Cliona by the Shore

I let myself in
   with the key of the kings and
   wrapped red ribbons
   around my poor head.
   'I thought you were dead,' said
   my mother.

I fired up at this and she waved me aside
   'I merely remark,' was her only reply

I heard on the news that the Temple had
   fallen.
   I am aghast at their simple faith
   and men search their words
   for slivers of meanings -
   shards and remnants
   of a truth they will hate.
   'You came home too late,' says my mother

The debt I repaid is burning a hole in my pocket
   For the cruelty of martyrs is mercy.

The wet grass smelt sweetly
   Giving me courage.

I willfully left there
and drove to the ocean,
but none of the fishermen
put out to sea.
'Are you leaving me?' asks my mother

I smiled in return and released her to fade.
   For I am the prophet of beauty decayed.
   We dwell by the shore now
   And bless the white thimble,
   the rue grows around us
   like weeds on a grave and the favour still warms us
   in cottage or cave.
   'We'll save the world later,' my wise mother says.

Death of the Hero

One note rising on the wind:
Piper play, the lament is called for.
Lower him down and softly keen -
Cu Chulainn's going to his rest.

Lady Emer, cry farewell.
The man is bruised and broken.
No token of your love will now
redeem Cu Chulainn from the grave.

Hang your heads, O noble beasts.
Hounds of Ulster, ye are bereft.
No master now, for he is slain
-there is no more Cu Chulainn.

Men of Ulster, faint and ill
bestir your voices in his name.
His fame should raise you from your cots -
Cu Chulainn cannot from the grave.

O grey world, no music now
no gay troop, no feasts or feis.
Dash the cup from kingly hands
Cu Chulainn cannot longer drink.

DEATH OF THE HERO

You could not face the man in life -
you feared to face him as he lay.
O men of Munster, hang your heads
Cu Chulainn beat you all at last.

Stand back, stay back and let
the birds of war attend his grave -
only they can follow now,
Cu Chulainn the hero as he goes.

Death of the Hero has been performed as part of a theatrical performance in Scotland and the USA.

Lament for Setanta

While "Death of the Hero," is a traditional lament for the iconic warrior, Lament for Setanta addresses the "death" of the child, sacrificed to the legend. Setanta the boy is subsumed into Cú Chulainn, the leader.

Setanta! Hard syllables of boyhood
    matured into *Cú Chulainn,* soft vowels
    sinister in their promise
    of war; lovely in their pledge of honour.

Setanta, young man of flawed ability
    ran with hounds and stepped lightly
    over the heather. Now how the ground
    trembles at the approach of the man!

Setanta, did your friends ever mourn you?
    regret the impulsive youth, the boy
    or were they all too dazzled by the warrior
    Cú Chulainn, Champion of Ulster?

Setanta, I will shed a tear for you, torn
    from the bosom of your family to run across
    foreign hills, losing in the chase the lad;
    to forge in his stead, the legend.

Crossings

Some roads
  lead to highlands, mountains -
  grand vistas
  and some from one side of mystery
  to another.
  Some show you continents
  but many
  simply the choice between
  open field and safe
  dark
  forest.

Meeting Bríd By Water

I looked across
  and saw
  a ribbon of silvered light
  and the first
  faint
  blush of rose dawn.
  This was Imbolg, the calling of Bríd -
  and She entered
  on a pathway of sparkling
  light.
  I looked across
  and my heart rejoiced
  at the soft tread of her
  across water.

Imbolg

She is cloaked in moments
   Glittering gems of rescued time
   on a gauze of twilight, in
   the grand stretch of an evening

Her eyes bring light to the day
   green as a new bud fighting
   for life beneath the hard cold soil
   reaching to greet the silvered day

Her voice is the poetry of the wind
   metred in short stanzas
   the breath of new life and fresh air
   as we call her into our homes

She perfumes the air with smoke
   burning it clean from the winter's decay
   it is a prayer to her, a blessing
   curling itself into the corners

O! Brid, you are the one that we need
   you are the dream that we cherished
   in the dark and the lean,
   in the belly of the turning year

Bean Chrosach

I am the Bean Chrosach
   A woman of fortune
   Your future in the palm of your hand

Nice cup of tea, dearie?
   Or the turn of a card -
   You tell them what they want to hear, he said

No, I do not, no –
   I tell them the bad,
   the sad things and good things, as may be

I tell them what the wind
   and the trees and the bees
   and the birds tell me to pass on

I tell them the truth and lie,
   I got it from the cards
   Or the tea or the lines or the stars

Yule at the court of Maeve

I left the city
   and traveled through the plains
   and found the forest
   of Warriors, among the forts of the
   kings.

The Warrior Queen, Maeve of the Sidhe
   beloved of the Hunter and
   favourite, blessed daughter of the Morrigan
   greeted me.
   I vowed never to return to
   the corruption of the free.

I fished on the shores of the Atlantic;
   I have prayed on the Mountain of
   saints.
   Late autumn now finds me dwelling
   deep in the forest, with those
   who escaped, like me.
   I have no suits and no favours.
   I walk in bare feet with the deer.

In the winter, I will pack my pelts

and furs, make me a gurney and load it.
I will pull it to the Court of the Tribes of the West.
I will unload it at the feet of Maeve
and beg her receive her daughter, and
I already know the pleasure I will see, in my mothers' eyes.

I will pass Yule there and stay until
  Imbolc.
  No more will I measure time by the glossy calendar of man. I will await
  the spring with a glad heart,
  and then,
  when the mountains shed their covers
  and the green rushes re-appear,
  I will gather my bow and my dagger
  and once more, to the Hunt again.

Breaking Faith With Aengus Óg

I fell out with the God of Love circa 2003 over some bad choices and composed this in retaliation:

I no longer love thee,
   Aengus Óg.
   I ll burn thee no more incense.
   I ll leave no meat nor mead nor gold;
   my faith in thee has grown
   stone cold.
   I no longer love thee, Aengus Óg.

Too many tears and
   sleepless nights;
   too many phone calls unreturned.
   My heart has burned and froze and crack'd
   and ached, for every lover
   lacked.
   I cannot longer stand the rack.

Too many faithless, fickle
   men
   with cruel intent and wand'ring eye;
   with hand and mind and deed have broke
   my soul and put it to

the Yoke,
and made me, but their secret joke.

No, no longer will I love and lose,
   nor wait until another choose:
   I no longer love thee,
   Aengus Óg -
   I'll burn thee no more
   Incense.

Apologies to Aengus Óg

Aengus had the last laugh.

Toast and Belgian Chocolate

We breakfast on toast and
   Belgian chocolate;
   dine on kisses,
   sleep on promises
   soft as feather beds.
   It's not meant to be this easy, you said.

I disagree. I have fought my battles
   and plead my case - Aengus owes me
   for the many nights of lonely heroism,
   stoic facing down of single combat.

We move in a shy dance
   through past and present;
   signpost failures,
   and flag our successes;
   with some aplomb

   lay both at each other's feet.

I remark His presence
   in the irony
   of our sudden being -
   laughing at our surprise
   and tricking us out
   in His favours, while we stare.

I owe Him an apology, unreserved
   for the simple pleasure I receive
   in the giving and receiving of a kiss
   warming cold lips before we leave.

Bealtaine

Bealtaine was first published in the Jane Raeburn Anthology and has been performed as a dramatic piece and public ritual several times.

Bealtaine

The fires were extinguished at dusk;
   doused, dampened, across the
   belly of the land.

The last inspiration of twilight,
   fading with the dying rays of sun
   denying the existence of hope.

The rushlights and candles
   standing in brown pots
   snuffed out with ruthless decision.

Breathless and wanton
   She welcomes the dark
   finding perfect acceptance.

A rapidness, daringness, derangement
   of wood on skinfulness, sinful the way
   they dance against the gathering night.

Cool breath of death
   against overheated limbs
   brushing against mountain ranges.

Hidden the contours of valley and hill
   From the eyes of greed and envy
   And on they dance still, heavy with desire
   Pausing with expectations
   refusing extolments of false praise
   insisting on the truth of cruelty.

Til light streaks and nudity is warmed
   By the rising sun, colour restored
   In a land overlooked

The mid-time, the time of forgetting
   The removal of knowledge
   The trampling of self.

Til light steaks and reawakens
   In a land unobserved, the tumultuous waters
   Unaltered in course by the reappearance of light.

And the union of dark and lucid
   Galvanizes the sleeping soul
   of rush bordered lake and pebbled beach

And the call of the curlew opens up
   The soft turf and heather of the marshy
   straights, straddling the west

slight lines of silver traverse
   the sleeping Eriu, the stretchmarks

of rebirth.

The Fires are relit at dawn, reborn
   with tongues of merriment
   sending messages across the face of god.

Rivers of silver this time,
   free-flowing, pushing the days out
   So that evening meets dawn.

Lughnasadh

Lugh among the people.

Deliberate, in measured steps,
   approaching the great circle
   leading the people to pray, with the sound of brass trumpets;
   Priest or Poet, calling us each to his own, filling our hearts
   with the beat of a bodhrán and the sound of the pipes made of thorn
   I am the dancer, lost in the rhythm of nature, dancing on the edge
   of the world, swinging out over chasms of infinity
   lit only by the ice cold stars.
   Singing a song I heard somewhere
   mourning the loss of a woman
   of infinite love. I am the Creator of words.
   I am the Fiddler. I am the moment when Summer ends,
   yet still the sun beats down and the Earth yields.
   I am the paradox, of Autumn beginning

Solstice

Solstice is an event often represented among pagans as part of some "Wiccan calendar wheel" or as a kind of national Djembe festival.

This poem springs from an attempt to express the moment of Solstice both as an astronomical event and as a spiritual one. The suspended moment provides opportunity; the place, Royal Tara, provides the Brí and Bua - the accompanying energy and context for any moment of spiritual intensity. Unlike other poems I have written, which are flights of imagination, this like "Dowsing" is a real event recounted in poetic language; an inversion of reality and imagination.

Solstice

1.
   Circular
   these are the paths we walk
   Spiral.

I turn inwards
   following the threads
   of a rambling thought

in the still-dark of dawn.
Once familiar shapes now
loom, catching me
unawares; opening my eyes
to their true nature
immutable, inscrutable;
more, suddenly, than the
gentle mounds, motherly breasts
undulations of Tara
I turn again
disoriented, in my own land.

II.

I am shaken
   my presumption is revealed.
   How I have said before
   I know these things
   I who missed the stark pride
   of Lia Fail; the cool aching
   slope of the mound?
   I who was used to run
   over the edge
   of what this new light shows
   to be a chasm?
   Dizzying heights and depths
   spinning in infinity

III.

I sink into knee-high grass
   my senses filled, my eyes

dazed. The light eats sky
til only day remains.
the veil has descended
as the dark recedes
and all around me-
familiar terrain, well loved
tracks, the geography of
Tara reasserts itself.
But I have glimpsed
an inner scheme; overlaid
the landscape of my soul
with the bones of this place.
I walk the spiral
from the Royal mound
to Eireann; in the bowels
of the earthworks, on the edge
of the ramparts
marveling.

IV.
As the full day blossoms
smiling on a motley group
of locals, pagans,
lost drunks and tourists
drums and voices raised
I struggle to reconcile
an eternal moment
an internal moment
with the careless gaiety
of an Irish feile in summer

that heartbreaking suspension
simultaneous dwelling
that - to me -
is Solstice.

Down by Ben Bulben

Down by Ben Bulben, the leaves are turning
   the russets are emerging
   triumphant over green, gold
   running riot, copper beeches
   glowing. Orange the wayside flowers
   and pale blue the sky -
   September has arrived.

Down by Ben Bulben
   As the road slopes to Leitrim
   the Glencar lakeside boasts
   colours fit to clothe a king. The crows
   startle black against
   the spread of the year's last finery
   a mantle of splendour
   as the sun crowns the day.

Snow in Dublin

This poem was written as part of my devotions as an Urban Pagan

You can keep your snow-capped mountains
   I can pass
on fields of virgin white.
The real power of snow is seen
on chimney stacks and pavements,
perfection silhouetted against a city skyline.
Ice on the locks
of the Canal;
Prim herbaceous borders
flaunting feather boas of powdered frost
sequined like housewives at Christmas.
Children freed from board and desk
run amok. Good old-fashioned amok.
There are no smells to rival
your neighbour's breakfast
cooking on a snowy morning.
Skies of leaden foreboding,
offset by central heating and
curried chips.
The fleeting pathos of a snow day
the knife-edge balance of work and
roads too snowbound for traffic

O! the thrill.
You can keep vistas of grandeur
nothing beats the slow and stately grace
of the 46A sailing past, unable to stop
on brakes too far gone for snowy roads

Swans and Chimney Stacks

Only in Dublin
   would two swans
   crossing the docks
   greet you in March

Light reflecting
   refracting the image
   of urban life
   and city living

hazy sun and
   smokey stacks
   a tall ship mast
   and two wild swans

Welcome to my city
   cosmopolitan
   21st century
   metropolis

Welcome to my city
   Viking territory
   mystical land
   mysterious port.

Dowsing

"Dowsing" was first published in the American Dowsing Journal; I have never discovered an iota of talent for dowsing in myself, despite many attempts.

Twitch! I think.
   Twitch, I beg.
   Stumbling over uneven ground
   trying to feel with rods,
   and see
   without looking
   and walk without falling face down
   in a cow pat.

I am a source of unlimited
   amusement
   to the man who can dowse.
   He was introduced in a flurry
   of West Cork accents
   and I am still not sure
   if he is Pat, or Aloysius or Maurice
   But he is one of these three

and his two brothers also watch,
ancient sprites with gleeful malice,
the Dublin bint in her dowsing infancy.

I am not getting anywhere.
   My Mother can dowse without effort
   my own hands are clumsy
   they can feel the note in a cello string
   but they are not open to the music
   that is water or energy.
   I feel the anger of failure
   I am not a good loser.
   I consider faking it
   but something tells me they would not
   be even slightly convinced.

I am not good at this.
   I listen humbly while Pat
   or Maurice or Aloysius
   tells me to relax, to practice
   to hold, to loosen, to be more aware
   to be less self-conscious.
   I vow to go home and walk
   the length and breadth of the park
   clutching these infernal rods
   of course, I don't-
   they sit as I write
   reproaching me from the sideboard.
   I may be destined never to unlock
   their elusive secrets.

Hidden Jester

Grief comes,
   in glancing blows
   stealing up at tangents -
   shards of promise, taut with loss,
   might have been, should have been.
   Nothing direct or clean;
   but sharp cuts and sudden hurts
   from shadowed corners.

Strange friend,
   thief, despoiler
   relying on one saving grace,
   one charity of memory, doled out.
   Taking more than giving;
   a parasite of living;
   poisonous flower, spreading
   like a weed.

Hidden Jester
   laying small traps
   that catch you unawares -
   the detritus of life, turned enemy

banal weapons that shard the heart
and once you start
you cannot stem the flow
and he has won.

The Jester

I went to see the Jester in her court
    she wore her tattered rags with pride, I saw
    pulled at the holes and gently sighed about
    the lack of courtly manners in the world.

I listened to the Jester as she sang
    her words ringing hollow in the halls
    "My cloak I wrap around me in great pomp"
    as she pawed the ragged edges with clawed hands

I asked the Jester if she ever wore the Truth;
    she eyed me, like a spider eyes its prey
    I say, It's not that hard a question, to be sure?
    She thanks me for my visit with a smile.

I would have pressed her further if I could
    she bandies words around like weaponry -
    forgiveness is a scalpel in her hands
    and justice is an axe she likes to throw

I wouldn't trade for all the gold you offer
    but the Jester is quite happy, I believe
    Our reunion was a success in her eyes
    She'll weave a song about it and I'll sing.

Ancestor

A poem for those left behind, from those who went before: Ancestor has in recent years become the centrepiece for funerary rites and for remembrance ceremonies.

If I should die tonight
   and my bones laid in the earth
   would my voice not be the wind
   and the sun my smile?
   I am the blood in your veins;
   all the lives I have lived
   have been, in this way,
   transmuted to new life
   flowing from your heart to mine.
   I am the beat of the Bodhrán
   and the touch of the line on water
   I am the thought unbidden
   the instinct that springs -
   If you listen not to me,
   then you ignore yourself,
   and silence your own voice.
   I am the string plucked,

ANCESTOR

the note quivering
the dream sung by voices
you remember from your cradle.
I am the silent watch of the nights
and the first breath of morning
because you carry me always in your heart

Lower me not

Lower me not,
   into a crimson mouthed coffin
   under mahogany covers
   a secret tucked away
   Lower me not
   into damp clay
   weighted down
   by marble grey

Set me ablaze
   set me free
   set me flying
   like a dying comet.
   Across the sky
   fling me, swing me,
   let the wind kiss me
   set me spiraling in flaming arcs.

LOWER ME NOT

float me away
   a petaled offering
   on a river of spices
   through red dusty land
   or rip me, expose me
   the bare bones of me
   spreadeagled on a table rock -
   part of the raven, or the wolf

Requiem

REQUIEM

This poem was composed many years ago in an emotional response to the attitudes of Nuns and Priests to us as young women. It was then published in an online publication in the noughties. A man immediately contacted me to say while he enjoyed my poetry in general, this one was obviously not Christian in nature and should be withdrawn.

I can only wonder what poetry of mine he read that made him think any of it was Christian in nature!

In Nomine Patre
   who art encountered
   in the skies on
   clouds with harps
   and cherub faced saints
   and the few women
   who art thought fit
   to be entered there
   Et Filis
   whom I hold personally
   to blame,
   for every slight
   and night I suffer
   in this female form:
   each sickly youth
   who ever wrote of
   this feminine
   in terms of sweet and soft -
   each woodwork class
   that was only meant for
   boys

Et Spiritus Sanctus
Sanctimonious
Git, tongues of flame
crying shame on my miniskirts and weekends away
and high heeled shoes and jobs
on building sites; on fights
and girls who
whistle in the corridors
of power
Amen!
In peace repose, rest and decay
Say no more, enough
was done in your name.
Abide in the past. RIP.

Night Chorus

A devotional poem to An Morrigan
    Across the last plains
    under leaden skies,
    the ground peat-brown beneath;
    Turf cutters pausing to point
    at the summers last black-breasted flight,
    across the dark eddies and whirlpools,
    the silver line of the river beneath;
    Over the wild heather of the stone hills
    from the Cairns of the west
    to the graves of the silent east.
    A black sunset, the death of a new day remarked.

Shrill and defiant in calling
    the passage of the long evening mourned.
    The gravel paths of the interlopers,
    darkened by the cloud of dark wings,
    stirred by the shadow of the future.
    The reminder that death precedes life,
    The smoke of the fires rising slowly;
    the wheel of the wing on the turn.
    The veil drawing over the midlands,
    the song of the night slowly silenced,
    the call of the dusk borne away.

Territory

First
   was the spear shaft

spiked in my soft flesh
   with anger and with fear
   and I first heard the word
   'mine'

After
   were many spikes
   cranogs and fences,
   ramparts and causeways
   pinpricks that tore

perforated the completeness
   of my soul
   and many voices shouted
   'mine'

soon after
   deep scars

gashes across the face of me
   a million hands all grabbing
   all tearing
   all shouting
   'mine'

All using part of me
   a sacred communion

throwing me like offal to pigs
   drawing lines through my
   energy
   all building boundaries
   all enslaving me
   all claiming me,
   'mine'

I contemplate
   spinning out of orbit
   into the ice-cold rind of space
   into the red-heat of a burning sun

into the wasteland of eternity
   and when their shouts have silenced
   point at the endlessness of time
   and tell them
   'mine.'

II

Dreams of Reality: At the Gate

Poems of Politics

Eriu Addresses the False Kings

Eriu Addresses was written for public use as a Rosc - an old Irish form of verse found throughout Irish literature from the Early Medieval period, used in battle magic, law and matters of public interest. It was composed in protest against a proposed meeting of men openly dedicated to supporting rape culture and oppression of women; these men called themselves "kings" which is a dangerous title to lay claim to in Ireland.

Their meeting was canceled and the reason cited - they were afraid of the women of Ireland.

Eriu Addresses The False Kings Of Ireland

As the False Kings attempt to impose themselves on the people, Eriu moves from Her seat to address the assembled crowd

False speaker, false leader, false man
    Born of a woman, unworthy of the honour
    Debased by your rejection of Her womb, Her heart
    Enemy to half the world
    Apostate to the other
    Liar and spreader of lies, like mould and decay
    Dead among men, unborn among women
    Unclean among the pure of spirit

Firenne rejects you
You are false and therefore unable to exist
You are the three marks on a king's cheek
Your ramparts fall before the anger of the Druids
And the Wise Women will make bread from the fire
Of your roof,
The earth rises against you
The stones and bones and blood of the land
Reject you and your band
Be they born of the land, they are undone
Found them shelter in this land, they are undone
If they visit this land, they are undone
The birds of the air, the food of the earth
The spirit of life, the Tuatha and their homes
The Tiarna and their laws, the Tír and its being
Turn from you, deny you, fast against you
The root of your name is poisoned in the ground
your stem is blighted and the ground salted against you
Your tongues fall silent, your limbs weakened, your fruit die untasted on the branch
And you are unmourned in the hour of your fall.
False speaker, false leader, false man.

Author's note This poem was subsequently published in the Journal Of Gods and Radicals – Edition, A Beautiful Resistance

Aisling

This poem was a prizewinner in the inaugural Listowel Writers Week John Murray competition. The brief was to express the demise of the Celtic Tiger and while many lamented the excess of the era, I wanted to remind us all that it broke the doom and hopelessness of the 80s and 90s in Ireland, and raised our expectations. It wasn't all bad. And also, our Old Lady has seen worse, it takes more than this to knock her out.

She came to me in a dream, an aisling of vodka
    Sat on the bed and said
    Howya,
    swinging last season's Hermés.
    "It's such a pity, isn't?" she said. "I was enjoying that."

The last time I saw her, she was an old woman.
    Not so well dressed, though she still wore green.
    The eyes were the same though, and the air.
    Ten thousand years will give you some dignity.

The party's over, I repeated the cliché.
    She gave me a look.
    Really?
    I could tell she was vexed
    "Don't *you* start, and all," she said. "I'm not finished yet."

She flicked her long hair, dark eyes defiant;
   I can hock the jewellery and sell the cars
   I can go back to ploughing that bloody green field
   I've a few tricks in my crane bag yet.

Where Once Stood Tribes

Where Once Stood Tribes was first published by Asia Geographic; it was donated to their "Tribes" edition which highlighted the vanishing world of Tribal peoples in Asia.

Where once stood tribes
   who rose and fell
   on the bounty of a living land
   soul and soil intertwined
   One blood, one heart,
   of one mind,
   muscle and sinew
   rock and tree

now stand deserts
   razed and mined
   farmed not free and filled
   with remnants of a glorious past
   now dismissed
   barbarous land
   savage land

   free land

Once here ran the young
   chasing after quarry
   wild whooping youth
   training for the fight
   with hunt and flight
   stone blow
   axe fell
   arrow flew

Once stood Warriors
   honour bound to those
   whose small lives fed
   whose small bones ground:
   love of warrior
   for the fallen enemy,
   so sweet in pain
   life in death
   alive in death.

Who can judge
   from these degenerate times
   the free and brave?
   Bearers of ancient honours
   honour of soul
   of strong arm
   of strong back
   of keen eye
   of fleet foot?

The Host of the Morrigan Marches Again

Written For Lora O'Brien, Author and Organizer of Morrigans everywhere

The recruitment drive was quietly done;
   stealthy *(by design)*
   signs were set, and entrails yielded omens.

Some of those conscripted in
   didn't even know they were
   til orders came and uniforms were donned.

"Onwards!" cried their leader
   sword drawn, and battle eye a-gleam.
   "Um, what's the plan?" one Private asked.

"I have a dream, " the curt reply. And
   no one asked again, for who can argue
   with the power of a well-placed Aisling?

She will be pleased, when She sees
   the standards flying and the cauldrons
   set again over flames -

the felling of great trees no longer
    acceptable, the ranks improvised
    with government papers and utility bills -

and the red gold of the setting sun
    over the smooth undulations of the land
    sets fire to visions of a Nation's pride.

The Host of An Morrigu marches once again
    though *wanders* might better describe
    some of its progress towards the field of carnage

while some dance and sing and others still
    sharpen pens and draw ink like blood
    from their own veins.

Still they are a war-band, and they will fight
    whatever weapons they choose
    in this world or the others.

Aylan

A three year old boy drowned off the Greek coast, trying to reach land with his family. The refugee crisis and the callous, self-serving response to it from the EU, and individual member states including Ireland, has been our single greatest moral failing as a society.

I dressed my son for school today
   I thought of Aylan
   I thought, as I wrote my child's name on his jumper
   Is this how they would identify him
   In the salt tears of the sea
   If we were at war
   If we fled?
   My youngest lies in bed
   Just as Aylan lies on the beach
   But mine is safe
   Because we won a lottery before birth
   Born on the right patch of spinning rock
   At the right time
   In the right skin.
   One hundred and sixty years earlier

I would crowd my children onto coffin ships
Ignore the taunts of dirty irish
Scrabble for work or scraps
or beg or steal or walk with bleeding feet
And they would tut at the state of us
The starving Irish.
In the veins of my children runs the blood
Of a mother who saved her two year old
From famine and death
By doing these things
And worse.
When I close my eyes
I see Aylan
But he has the face of my own child.

The Economics of Power

Ní thuigeann an sách an seang;
   the well fed do not understand the lean.

The rich cannot guess the inner life
   of shacks and shanty towns.

The fat of the land, the smooth cream
   covers the gristle of life with plump meat.

How can they know the pangs of empty bowls?
   Ní thuigeann an sách an seang - but they set the prices all the same

The Madness of Women

You see black
   I see a spectrum of invisibility
   the myriad shades of the dark rainbow
   like the spread of raven's wing
   under the yellow mellowness of an Autumn Moon

You see rain
   I see diamonds of potential crashing
   soft tears of heaven salty with life
   worlds contained within, the moment of creation
   plummeting toward earth to burst open into growth

You see mountains
   I see the slumbering form of beauty
   curvaceous limbs caressed in silken folds
   breasts marked by the fall and rise of shadows
   ropes of silver rivers binding Her to us

You hear the wind
   I hear the Song that called us into being
   undulating notes of power, secret cadences
   voices lifted, speeches spun, prayer uttered
   all human history and earth's in one voice

THE MADNESS OF WOMEN

You see only what you want to see
   I see all there is to be seen
   You think the world can be reduced to numbers
   and you call me mad?

What Shall You Teach Your Son?

WHAT SHALL YOU TEACH YOUR SON?

This poem was written as part of a wider dialogue with feminists and allies about rape culture, misogyny and fourth wave feminism. What we teach our boys is important – teach them to respect women as inherently entitled to respect, not as Madonnas or virgins or "good girls." Teach them to take responsibility for their own actions. I have two sons, and they will learn this at my knee.

How do we fix this shit?
   Let us start with what we teach our sons
   Yes you, my innocent little man;
   If you ever lay your head next to mine
   And whisper that you have hurt, degraded or demeaned
   Some woman
   Any woman
   Any girl
   The old one. The ugly one
   The pretty flirt. The one whose skirt
   Is too short or blouse too low.
   The silly one. The shy one. The odd one.
   The one who was mean. The one who said no.
   The one who passed out.
   The one your mate said was loose.
   Any one of them
   You will feel the power of your mother.
   You will quickly learn that I am woman, too.
   But I love you, my son.
   So I will teach you first
   No means no.
   Drunk means no.
   Unconscious means no.
   Uncomfortable means no.

But before that I will teach you
She is entitled to wear, speak, like, dislike, walk, drink, think, live
How she pleases.
And before that I will teach you
There are just people.
Not a war between sexes.
Just people.
You are people.
She is people too.
And when some people try to make you forget that, I will teach you
To say -
No.

Ar Scáth a Chéile

Ar Scáth a chéile a mhaireann na daoine.
   People live in the shadows of each other;
   We are each of us the shelter,
   The roof that abides against the storm;
   The shade that thwarts the harsh sun.

The land does not ask the rain
   Whether it was from the Wicklow streams
   Or the mighty Shannon or the unimaginable torrents of the Amazon
   Was it drawn? It merely drinks it in.

That we live under the shade of each other,
   Is the only truth we need,
   And our only choice. Offer leaky roofs and grudging shade.
   Offer our whole presence and the run of the place.
   Whichever we choose, we will receive.

The Dublin Rosc

Composed against the racist, far right riots in Dublin. Dublin is the birthplace of the Rising, the blood of patriots stain these streets. To dishonour their legacy is a dangerous business.

By the hallowed ground of martyrs
   I call to the beating heart of my city -
   Awake!
   Your wrath upon them,
   the traitors damned by their own fires.
   Gather now, ye hosts, and defend
   this, our Mother
   from those without honour
   without clan, without name, without price.
   They are the broken laws of hospitality
   They are the stain of cowardice
   They are the three blemishes of the cheek
   Awake now, our city
   founded by The Foreigners
   the open gate to our freedom
   the rallying call of our nation.
   My City, My Heart, My Soul
   Rise now Dubliners
   Come to our aid O Deise
   Send us the sons of the kingdom and the daughters of Royal Meath

The Rebels raise the Banner
and the stony fields throw themselves to our cause
for we are the Tuatha and we do not fall
Anna Livia herself approaches, to sweep away their lies
for She is our home and our safety
Dishonour done in her name is our shame
The Laws grind them down
The Laws break them down
The Laws scourge their backs
Awake! Great Lady, Awake
and show them who you really are,
on this hallowed ground of martyrs.

Sparks

Outside a semi-D in Dublin
   Holding placards. Disturbing the
   Innocent sleep of a baby.
   Out out out, a chant so negative
   In its echoes of pub fights
   (Take this outside, I'll bleedin smash ya)

Outside a hotel, earmarked for refugees
   (*Earmarked for homeless families*)
   They don't care about reality. Instead
   They give people nightmares about large men
   Undocumented. Illegal. How does a person become illegal
   (*Unless by colour or creed?*)

It didn't start here. It started with rumours
   That Christmas trees were banned because it might offend
   Or that women were not safe (we're not but Irish men were to blame
   Not your nameless, faceless bogymen)
   And all the times you didn't say anything
   When someone repeated the lies
   (*They get houses, cars, money, while we work – the same they used to say –*
   Single mothers, junkies, the unemployed, the Travellers)

Ah here.

They carry burning torches but -
  Did *you* light the flame?

Edda's Poem

For Dr. Edda Nicolson and for all those who battle mansplaining, patronizing, keyboard warriors. Edda is one of my heroes – clever, kind and quite possibly our future Overlady.

The Problem With Women

I post about issues, many feminist in tone
    Abuse of the female, inside the home
    or out on the streets in full view of all
    Or insidious lessons that make us feel small
    and I say every time not all men do this
    a line in my stories some men seem to miss
    and I say that the male is vulnerable too
    I say men are mainly good, and it's true.
    But then the replies start derailing the thread
    as some men read things I never actually said
    Answer accusations I didn't actually make
    argue the point for argument's sake
    I can talk about women broken and battered
    I can post about young girls whose dream have been shattered
    Without needing instruction from men who feel slighted
    You're not like that? Good. I'm fucking delighted.

EDDA'S POEM

Stop telling me that and read what I wrote
open your hearts and start to take note
because some of your kind are doing these acts
Don't be defensive just be aware of these facts
Give your opinion without the lecture. I'll listen
and I'll happily learn if there's something I'm missing
But in return when I point out your own oversight
don't call me a feminazi for daring to be right.
shrugging off debate with an injured defense
"Oh! The trouble with women is they take such offense."

Pussy Riots or Ailurophobia in Russian Life

The conviction of the three members of feminist Russian collective Pussy Riot is a disgrace and a challenge to feminism worldwide. It is also yet another attack on secularism, free speech and the rights of the artist. Ailurophobia is the irrational fear of pussies. Or cats.

Three of the cats who stood
   iconoclastic in their ritual,
   worshiping at the alter
   of free speech, and expression,
   obscenely repressed by
   the powers that be;
   three of these pussies
   are to be caged,
   declawed and toothless
   in a system long decayed.

Trolley busses and scaffolds
   are okay, it seems, for girls

   in balaclavas or women shouting
   the odds, but not a church,
   oh no, women's voices should not
   be raised in a church.
   It's nothing to do with politics you understand
   -it is their bold bad lack of respect for Him.
   (not him, Putin, but the other
   God of Russian politics.)

Burn your flags, my lovelies,
   far far better than fiery bras.
   Bite back, shout and torch the churches,
   roast them on a spit of lampoon –
   there is no place for the feminine divine
   Among the patriarchs of Russian life.
   Three cats jailed by frightened men
   and an apathetic nation, still the Party's bitch.
   Come! Let's be Hooligans, all, and light the way.
   Start by saying, today, I am Pussy Riot.

Another Angry Black Woman Speaks

I'm white, Irish, privileged and middle class, educated and while I'll never be rich, I've never suffered true poverty. That is my disclaimer, because whenever anyone writes about someone else's experience, someone else's point of view, they risk bringing a patronizing layer of filter to the issue. I can't say I know what it is to be a woman in a developing country. I know what it's like to experience discrimination for being Irish or female, but I don't know what it's like to experience daily racism, at first glance, in a million insidious ways. It's not my place to speak for black women; my sisters in feminism share many experiences with me that we can freely explore but I will never know how it feels to be them any more than someone else can say they "know" what it was to be Irish in Britain in the 80s. It's not my place to pretend I do.

But a lovely friend shared her frustration at the following and unruly poetry made itself in my head and I wrote it down and now I rely on her charity, and yours, to allow it stand, with the above in mind. She graciously consented.

Inspired by Kazi – another of my heroes. A woman of infinite wit and soul, and generosity.

Another Angry Black Woman Speaks (*And Makes Us All Uncomfortable*)

She pauses.
   Don't think I'm being aggressive, it's not that -
   I'm not saying you are the same, I'm not -
   Just that – one more person dead for being Black
   In the wrong place, at the wrong time? How can that happen?
   And yes I know not all police/white/insert your demographic
   Are like that, I know you've never done it,
   But it's hard to read and watch and fear and think
   What the hell is going on? And then
   When I talk to white friends, I see them stiffen
   Instead of listen, And it's the body language,
   the expression

The veiled reception of my words that says
   Oh no, another (she's such a, so very much a)
   I can see it coming
   "..Another Angry Black Woman."

She stops, and sighs. I know, I say tentatively
   Well, obviously I don't know, but I can glimpse
   If a woman talks at all, passion is hysteria
   Emphasis is aggression
   Strong words are criticism/harsh/giving out
   The dreaded
   "going on and on about it" -
   And I can see, from over here, how that is amplified
   For non-white, or poor, or gay
   And our friends agree, oh my god yes
   They say,
   I can totally see your point.

We move on,
   The topic tactfully, skillfully changed

Lighter moods prevail, we rail no more at fate.
But later, I get a call / text/ pm
"Omfg what did you make of that?
Why was she going on about it to us?
I've never been racist! I don't see colour, you know that!!
She made us all uncomfortable, and after you left
We were all talking, you know the way
She used to be a laugh but don't you think…
I don't like to say it
But hasn't she become…"
And the words are unsung, hung by hesitation
But I hear them so loudly they scream.

"Another angry black woman," - that's what they mean

See Me

Written as part of a series of poems during the Irish Marriage Equality Referendum.

See me, says Mary
   Born and bred in a rural town
   daughter of fields and grey stone walls
   See me, for I am a vote
   I am a choice, I am a new day dawning

See me, says John
   Under the glow of a street lamp
   Son of the city, the pavement and street
   See me, for I am a vote
   I am the future, I am the morning reborn

See me, says Dolores
   I may be old, but I can remember
   I have seen changes you can't imagine
   I am the past, but before I go
   the future is mine to secure for the young

See me, See me, for we have decided
   never again to close our eyes
   never pretend that our friends or our neighbours
   should live as we do, should live in the dark

should live without love, invisible hearts

SEE ME. For I am an ally
   and I will not let you silence them again
   those you ignore, I will acknowledge
   those you silence, I will shout out their names.
   You should see me coming, for I am a vote.

This Poem Has No Planning Permission

In protest at the attempted removal of a Pro Equality mural during the 2015 Marriage Equality Referendum.

This Poem Has No Planning Permission
    This poem is constructed
    unstructured
    and without
    planning permission.

It advocates a YES vote.
    I asked no permission.
    The artist can advocate what he wants
    and so can I

And I add, without permission
    an extension
    The bully is not oppressed
    when we make him stop bullying
    Giving others equal rights
    does not oppress you

This poem has no planning permission
    This poem is a YES vote

Vote Early and Often

I do not see, what makes me
  more worthy to be wed,
  than Annie and Jacyntha,
  or Maurice to his Fred?
  I possess no greater intellect
  Nor higher moral ground;
  No secret way to perfect love
  Have I or my ilk found.
  We row and fight and hurt and bleed
  And break and tear asunder,
  We heal the same, we love the same
  And when we're six feet under
  We'll all make bones, we'll all make dust
  And twill be hard to say -
  Which of us was wed or not,
  And who was straight or gay.
  So while we live and breathe we draw
  And the sun yet shines above ,
  Let us all be equal in one thing -
  The beauty of our love.
  If your heart holds within
  one single spark of joy,
  It matters not what fans the flame -
  The sight of girl or boy.

All that counts, is if that face
Brings solace to your life.
And if you long to call that name
Husband mine, or Wife.
So May fifteenth we all must join
To vote for all our sakes!
Vote early and vote often for
The difference marriage makes.

III

Dreams of Reality: By the Fireside

Poems of Community

At Work, My Grandfather

The epitaph "Scents of Incense" was composed by Fr Herman Nolan CP, written for my Grandfather Charlie Byrne, a Luthier and restorer of musical instruments. It is inscribed on his headstone, where also rests my father Charlie Byrne, whose life was similarly dedicated to music.

Scents of Incense, Glue and Varnish Cease;
   Perfect O Lord, thy instrument of Peace.
   Fr Herman Nolan CP

I saw my Grandfather at work,
   bent. He was old by then
   and white haired, my father
   dark and upright.

I watched the old man
   handle wood like it was
   his lover; all his tenderness
   and poetry in the making

of a single rib - to

play Eve, I suppose
   to some Violin.
   He had Pianist's hands

like a lady's at the tips
   but hard and calloused
   at the palm. He used to
   work, in the fields at

Summer and at Autumn
   and he had cleared land
   himself and stood shirtless
   in the sun

And worked through the rain.

ii

Now he was where he had belonged
   in his own father's place;
   his craft he plied, to my child's
   eyes, with consummate grace.

I smelt the incense
   and he told me the glue
   was jelly - that was the story
   I have always remembered.

The image of him frail
   in gone from my mind;
   of his time with us in sickness
   i remember only that

AT WORK, MY GRANDFATHER

Mammy and I once cleaned his room
   and I sat on the stairs
   and cried, when they said
   he had gone, and meant "died."

But I remember
   I saw my grandfather at work
   in a room, surrounded by
   shavings, and the smell of wood and glue.

Pilgrimage

For my friend Mael Brigde, and a memorable day spent with one foot in the past.

The day of Pilgrimage began, as all should do
   in the company of a rebel, the woman who threw
   class and status to the winds, for Ireland and the poor.
   Where once a hospital stood, stood she
   glorious in her stern beauty, and we her acolytes
   finding comradeship with others who sought her out.
   Constance greeted us, and we laughed, the best way
   to make penance for the past.

Our Croagh Patrick, our Camino Way
   led us to a red-bricked, respectable bastion
   on the northside of Dublin, where a school covered
   the remains of a place, where spectres held sway -
   the legacy of the dead to the living.
   In sunshine, we found a tree – contemporary
   of your ancestors, sentinel over their memories
   and we paid respect. Some healing was done, some
   minor miracle of existence, of defiance, of endurance.

We made our way back to the car, and he asked
   Where to next? A bridge near Pheonix Park, searching for
   The Dublin Union (whisper the word, *Workhouse*) and

finding some solace that the affluent, the young
The vigorous and free, had eradicated its foundations.
We, without saying it, were glad.

But there was one spot left, one Calvary to find
   On a road we were afraid no longer existed
   Our only marker that there should be a hill.
   Dublin Traffic was a dragon,
   poor husband behind the wheel a valiant knight.
   Shall we give up? Hung the words on the air,
   reluctantly agreed. Until a chance, a sign,
   writing on the wall from the sages of the Corporation

- *This is it!*

Pure chance rewarded faith, our own resurrection of hope
   and you traveled the very path that shaped the lives of
   those who shaped your own. We laid no wreaths and took
   no selfies but tired and joyous, set out home.

Irish Cowboys

First published in the Ezine "Prairie Poetry" this is one of my strangely popular poems – I liked it but never imagined it would strike a chord with anyone else. Instead I was gratified, if bewildered, over the years to find it shared, republished and commented on favourably online and in print. It also garnered some emails – most very kind and pleasant but one particularly odd one from a man who told me how he would rewrite it and how I should have phrased it. I shamelessly trolled him by immediately replying as if his version was mine and mine his – he was not amused. This is for you, strange and inappropriate man, out there somewhere telling women how to write properly!

A poem of childhood

The wild west for us
   was never the stone walls
   and fragments of land between them
   the ragged, wild, bog-spawned
   west of Ireland
   It was a topography, a dialect, a code
   as familiar as our parents
   or our national tongue
   gleaned from Television, old movies
   dog-eared paperbacks.

IRISH COWBOYS

We were born in Dublin
but we all, each one,
roamed the wild prairies
hunting buffalo in our souls
spat tobaccy and smoked Marlborough
walked bowlegged - howdy pardner -
or grim and gimlet-eyed, we eyed the
scorching sun
talking in monosyllabic knowing exchanges
about drought, and cattle dying, and crops failing
thwarted in our childish hearts by
near incessant rain
and insolent verdant green.

What I gave up for New Year

How many years have I parroted
   that I would give up the usual:
   give up the fags and lose weight?
   Drink less, walk more?
   This year I am trying
   for newer and less banal
   brighter and more imaginative
   new year's demands.

I will give up
   people who are bad for me
   I will eschew their vision of me
   that binds me, limits me.
   I will renounce their prejudice of me
   the way I am diminished by their
   narrow and self serving lies.
   I will give up
   their sense of my failure
   their disappointment at me
   the way they wanted more from me
   the way they expect so little of me
   I will avoid, the saturated fat of life
   the easy sense of usefulness that comes

from being all things to all people
and I will accept
that tough decisions make enemies.

I will resolve to
   be more of me and less of them
   to put me first, and mine,
   ahead of everyone else and theirs.
   I will make time that is mine,
   and remove it from the claws
   of duty or commitment,
   squander it gloriously
   in half hours of decadence
   and no longer apologize,
   no more say sorry
   to people who see kindness as
   weakness.
   I will be ruthless in my giving
   as in my taking
   stopping when I need to, refusing
   to have gratuity
   redefined as obligation.
   And if they want to take, let them say
   please and thank you.

I resolve on this, to remember
   each day has its own beauty
   distinct from the place it left
   and irrelevant to its destination.
   I promise myself, that i have
   no less and no more than my rights
   and will not accept the judgment
   passed on me by others, whose

failed agendas seek me out,
to hold me up, to expose and denude.
Instead I will clothe and adorn
myself if no one else will.

Send Up A Flare, My Lovelies

We are all of us
   Lone currachs, isolated naomhógs
   Wandering the treacherous seas
   Peering into the dark night.

Send up a flare
   Let your distress signal be a star burst
   Shed light on yourself
   So we may see your plight.

When you do, you create
   Light by which to see and be seen
   And if we all do, we become a fleet
   Under a banner bright.

Saving Sylvie

This is a poem about the impossibility of knowing some people, and the cloaking of ambiguous intent by good deeds. It was first published in the PPP Anthology Pagan Paeans, and subsequently in anthologies in Ireland and the UK.

I was restored by the sight of her
   my bustling nursing Sylvie with long smiles,
   and I told her so.
   She shook her head, still smiling.

I am the last patient in a ward
   of ten; the others have been cured
   and moved on, to families
   and welcomes home.
   I am the death head's at the feast.
   No wonder Sylvie looks so glum.

If I weren't here the rows of
   starch and snow would be unbroken.
   I would hold court on the balcony

be wheeled ceremoniously, one last time
to doctors' jokes and nurses' smiles.
I would if I could but I won't, you know.
I stay here just to spite you, Sylvie.

I hear they are remodeling the ward
   where will they put me, I wonder?
   In my darker nights I fantasize.
   I am in a broom closet,
   just me and the shelves
   and Sylvie comes to pick up some bed linen
   and winks, woman to woman.

I am in the garden,
   overgrown with ivy,
   a living statue, a grey memorial
   Comes my doctor with a bouquet
   and behind her with a wreath,
   the ever hopeful Sylvie
   and she sighs, to see the empty line
   on the headstone she donated.

In the bright day, I think
   I may have misjudged her. I
   love her even; like I love
   the nectar in these tubes.
   Ah, I am restored by the sight of her
   galled, and reminded of my decreasing
   and I told her so.
   She just shook her head, still smiling.

Secrets of The Dead

When I couldn't bear it anymore
   the nurse pointed to the glass door
   and said:
   the grounds are lovely
   at this time of year.
   I didn't like to tell her
   I was dying for a cigarette;
   there were quite a few inside,
   gutted from the same.

I found a bench, private on a gravel walk
   and tried to breath and inhale
   all at once. I saw an old man eyeing me
   greedily following each smoky tendril;
   Jaysus, I could taste that, he whispered
   and I nearly offered him one.
   But the nurse stood sentinel on my manners.

Pleasantries suspended, down he sat;
   flannel under duffle; woolen hat.

It's not the illness that I mind, he said
it's the dying; and he choked and wheezed
with mirth, gallows humour being in fashion here.

D'ya know what, he said, I hate the thought of them ones
   pawing through my private things.
   I left a letter in my bedside drawer-
   I wish I'd burned it long ago. They'll
   see my dirty underwear; What will they think
   of the magazines? I could weep, he confided,
   I'll die of the embarrassment;
   this set him off again, asthmatic chuckling.

We were driven back inside with the rain;
   I took up my accustomed place again
   and tried to think of clever things to say
   and visiting time dragged on -
   while I made a mental inventory of
   underwear and poetry and love letters
   and tampons and diet sheets and tried
   to calculate how fast they'd burn.

Making Amends

You used honeyed words
   I used wildflowers in a glass jar
   It seemed mad to be at odds
   while bees and flowers and summer sun
   conspired to make us smile

All childish grief dispersed
   games and play resumed
   our chubby arms entwined
   like honeysuckle ropes that bind
   our idols to their throne

And now I wiser am
   and hear beneath your tone
   to all the use you have for me
   to all the use you ever had
   had I but ever known

And now I pride my adult heart
   for adult sins to see
   yet as a dupe in innocence

in summer games and pretty play
My heart was far more free

The Old Familiar Faces

It's a long road to come
   from seventeen and scared
   to thirty odd and counting.
   It's a long hard road
   paved with sliding rules
   and passed milestones
   and unremembered anniversaries.
   Desk diaries littered with cruel reminders;
   friends I never see
   and promises broken before they were made.
   Here and there a scribbled note;
   a jotted down reminder of the roads
   not taken, sometimes not even glimpsed
   and through it all
   a handful of names
   like the solid, recurring bass note of a drum
   beating like a heart.

Make up your mind

So when I saw it -
   was introduced to it, like,
   I wasn't terribly impressed.
   But what could I say?
   I wasn't listening, it was not I?

It was solid,
   much more there than I
   had imagined -
   much more final
   more respectable.

Although - if I am honest -
   it was obscene. That it was, at all,
   was
   offensive.

Or am I just
   panicked?

Let it go

It remains to be seen

For some reason that sounds
   fanciful and fun
   Like,
   we can decide it all later
   It doesn't really matter
   It's not all that important

Whereas I know
   it can't be postponed.
   I can see, how it would be
   awkward
   become a point of contention
   if we were too
   laissez faire.

I compose myself.
   Literally I make myself up.
   I invent stanzas, so that when
   I am asked
   I may answer.
   This is interminable. Hard benched,
   hard pressed. I wait.

I suppose in the face of this;
   it all really is
   academic.

Making Links

Making Links

A poem in three parts

Decide now

1.

When She called
   I had my hands in washing up,
   up to the elbows
   hair falling in drips
   face hot and sweaty

2.

Is it oak or
   something lighter?
   what lining?
   I am winning the war
   on grease and remains -
   I do not wish to be thrown
   back into the heated debate.

Let someone else decide.

I am paralyzed
   in the face of brisk
   efficiency;
   left swimming a bubble
   prone to explosion
   ready to pierce myself
   and be consumed again
   by the whole.

There were several
   points raised that could
   be good or bad, depending.
   And some chit chat.
   I got off the phone lightly.

Stolen

Lately he has thought of stolen moments,
   of childhood's missing hours -
   of sneaking past the guardians of his age and sex
   and holding to the innocence he felt once
   was worth the loss.

But if his heart should wander
   where will it go?
   What is there for its sweet enduring hurt?
   What went before, is gone, was never reached and is no more
   and all paths returning stand in silence-
   unpassed.

On stony ground, You fall like rain

When I walk the hard path
   and stray, distracted by storm clouds
   you walk with me.
   I know it is your hand that
   pulls me back, steers me towards
   grass verges.

When I am blinded by the sun,
   and fear I will not find my way again
   you call my name.
   It is your voice I recognize
   over the howling winds and
   screaming gales.

When I can find no rest or shade
   it is you who shelters me, like an
   Oak tree.
   I am safe with you, my love -
   for you fall on stony ground
   like rain.

By Your Presence Are You Known.

For Paula, for endless kindness; one of the rocks of my life. Sister in law, and second Mammy to my boys, no one better embodies the value of a kind heart to any community.

You will ask, or be asked someday
   What good have you done?
   What purpose, in this shifting world
   What weight did you place upon the scales?
   You cannot answer for yourself
   You'll never guess the moments
   Only others can tell the tale
   Of acts and omissions filed in your name
   But like golden coins they'll pile;
   Solid, worthy, generous, tangible,
   Each one with a testament affixed
   And each of these will start with this
   By your presence - three glorious words.
   By your presence, we were comforted
   By your presence, we were fed
   And burdens lifted, hard times eased

By your presence - tangled threads unbound,
Problems solved and time reclaimed
Tea and biscuits, time and thought
And always laughter, always some moments joy.
There will be volumes written and declared.
Each one of a kindness kindly given
Each one shining in the deepening dark
A line of light to lead you home.
You, you wear this lightly as you go
But by your presence are you known

Late Coffee

For James Owens. We still miss you.

You were there.
   In the smile when someone
   (could have been me.
   Allegedly.)
   wore the plastic gown -
   a mournful clown.
   You were there.
   in the moment you insisted
   on sitting up
   on getting out of bed.
   That old defiance, that bold man.
   You were there.
   In the pallid light
   over late night coffee
   in the echo of other times
   in brighter places.
   You were there.
   In the glint of an eye
   when we discussed the state

of the Irish nation
after the Black Prince, and you nodded.
You were still there.
When I left
you were still there.

For my husband, Poems that are not Valentines

1. *At Table*

I sat with you
   at table. Among friends
   we broke bread
   and your hand reached for mine.

Sup wine from my cup,
   steal sweets from my plate;
   All good things I have
   I offer to you, serve them up.

Are your cheeks flushed?
   or is it candlelight and fireside -
   the heat of the hall?
   or is it my touch, cooler than air…

I sit beside you
   at table. We are blessed
   in each other and friends
   and joined by merry words.

2.
This of Small Virtues.

There are things that endear you to me,
   strange items that hang in a wardrobe or
   lurk on shelves, shyly advertising you.
   The books on weight loss, gathering dust
   beside fantasy and sci-fi, testaments to your
   all too human frailty; the books on
   love and self, incongruous in a male library
   besides the Cosmos and Relative Physics.
   The way you embrace science and all
   the oddest facts of our tenuous existence on
   this planet; where you maintain mankind are
   monkeys in jumpers, but you are openhearted
   towards magic and the unexplained.
   These are the unresolved equations of your nature
   secrets that ambush me as I tidy away, or unpack bags
   riddles to the sweet core of your nature
   open only to me, only here, in our home

3.
This is not a Valentine

For a start it's two days late
   and will not rhyme.
   This is not a paean to one day
   to flowers or cards (ours unexchanged,
   unwritten, stolen and returned)
   I say again, this is not a Valentine.

This is not a Valentine;
   it is a hymn to mundane days,

FOR MY HUSBAND, POEMS THAT ARE NOT VALENTINES

days without titles and nights
without expectations; when a weary
hand stirs a bottle, takes a turn,
loads a wash, puts on dinner.
No, this cannot be a Valentine.

This is not a Valentine.
   No flowery verse would stoop
   to describe the loving act of hoovering
   or the romantic gesture of sweeping.
   No flowers are delivered, when a cup of tea
   is made and handed over with a kiss.
   No, No Valentine is this.
   This is not a Valentine.
   They'll never teach this poem in school,
   this ode to daily love. A kind word,
   a compliment unearned, a gentle touch.
   The heroic act of doing more than your share;
   to quietly care. Ah no, this is no Valentine.
   It is a poem of love

Love letters from a Busy Life

Hi, it's me
  I'm sorry that I haven't been in touch
  I see you every day, morning and night
  so why write? well, our time is short
  I seem to say hello, goodbye and sometimes
  in between, a hurried I love you
  but oh! it's not enough, my dear.
  Here in my head we talk all the time
  like we did when we were leisure rich.
  I itch to tell you all the details of my day
  and every way in which you touched them,
  lightened them, help me carry the load.

Is there room
  for love letters of the old type, the ones
  that fill the spaces in a busy life? Recount
  the dreams and hopes and fears of every day
  renew the links that bind us to our life
  and say, I would not live any other story
  walk any other path, fight for any other cause
  but you? You are my star, my stone, my roots
  and all there is to praise in heaven or on earth.
  You may not know this, but it's written there,

in shopping lists and texts about dinner -
whenever you read between the lines, it's there.

The committee for the Formation of Pagan Creation theories

For An Fianna, the best of community.

The scene: a darkened amphitheater,
   the centre stage bare but for the lone poet,
   the spotlight his at last.
   He raises soulful eyes to heaven and quoth he
   'In the beginning, you see
   there was this god called He
   and She was his wife. In boredom
   they created their own offspring,
   and thus it all began'

The muttering from the back grows louder-
   'Ballcocks! ' a learned colleague calls.
   Standing with the righteous wrath of
   six halves and two chasers
   'In the beginning there was the Great Mother Cow,
   and She created the Great Bull

THE COMMITTEE FOR THE FORMATION OF PAGAN CREATION THEORIES

by whom she had the Heifers of Plenty
everyone knows that'

'What? '
   the elegant repartee of the Lady Principle
   of the Esteemed College of Bards and Ovates
   interjects with her customary pith.
   'That shit? you think that's how it all began?
   My good man, you obviously forget
   We bards know it best. Danu and Dagda
   carried the world in a bag
   til their Bowling night,
   and they needed a strike to stay on top of the league
   And we are hurtling through space as a result,
   our mission is to win them first place.'
   Togas flapping, she is soon drowned out
   by the combined wrath of the Roman school
   with some support from the Greeks
   who are chanting 'Zeus' and making rude gestures
   indicating virility; Homer has Plato on his shoulders
   and both are trying to headbutt
   the Master of the College at Byzantium.
   In the melee,
   the Egyptians manage to shout
   something about dung beetles laying eggs in the sky
   and ugly big jackal-headed mothers.

The Amazonian tribes politely submit their views
   ignoring the vulgar jeers of the Phoenicians
   who smile the other side of their faces
   when the Norsemen decide they can't hear over them
   and decide to make a stand for public manners
   mainly on dung beetles heads.

Snorri Snugglesbum, Master Saga writer, challenges the hall
to prove it was not Odin, on a Tuesday, in the Library, with the
candlestick.

At last the dust settles, another robust debate
   abated. The Committee for the Formation
   of Pagan Theory of Creation
   surveys the scene with complacent eyes -
   'Well that was interesting ' The chairman sighs happily
   'Same time next week, lads?
   and someone else can bring the biscuits'

Transparent Years

For Ronan MacAonghusa

25 years ago
   On the concourse of UCD
   or hanging in the students union
   we were arrogant and lost
   in impossible measures

Transparent in our voices
   ideals worn with cynical pride
   tilting at dragons and chasing dreams
   angst and alcohol, side by side

25 years ago,
   you became a sentinel in my life
   prompting me when I stumbled
   one of the foundations
   of who I am.

We have both made our journeys
   in miles, in thought, in dream or deed
   each one ending in our reunion.
   Friendship it seems, is our only need.

Ladies Day

For Brenda Ryan

August in Dublin
   for her, was hats
   shoes and other
   sartorial excesses.
   But mainly hats -

Ladies day at the RDS
   sore shoes on inexperienced feet
   I complained but she laughed -
   Suffer for fashion, ladies!
   The rituals of ladyship

She took seriously
   played by the rules.
   once she made
   a lime green hat
   She was Hitchcock cool

With a passionate eye
   I remember most
   How she enjoyed it all

Sit Here

This is a poem dedicated to my friend Emer Ferns, who always makes room for someone to sit.

I heard on the news, those dreaded words of childhood
   "Back to school," the death knell of summer, the last nail
   in the coffin for the halcyon freedoms of our youth;
   I heard it and thought, it's September – remember! remember
   when that meant schoolbags and books and copies and pencils
   and suddenly thought, how long have I known her?
   How many years? How many seasons, since that first Autumn,
   how many days, since that first day of a new school year?

I walked in, my usual self; constrained by my lumpiness and
   dumpiness. I walked in and paused. My usual tactic was to
   see where there might be a seat – unobtrusive, unwanted, unlikely
   to offend anyone else. Perhaps on the edge of a group, that way I could
   occasionally, if the omens were good, turn and talk or share a joke –
   as long I didn't push my luck. I couldn't see a seat.
   I saw her. She smiled and pointed to the seat in front. She had already
   found a niche, made a friend, settled in. She pointed to a seat and then to
me.

I don't remember sitting down. I don't remember the first halting chat.
   I remember laughing. If I had to sum up the next thirty years, my friend,

her spirit, I would say…I remember laughing. There's no end to her laughter,

her good nature. She is kind. Everyone who meets her, says that. She is kind.

She has a knack with us oddballs, she is Mamma to us all. She has a way of making you feel as if you belong. She has made me feel that for thirty years, while I did my best to cast myself adrift, while I spun aimlessly out of orbit. I never knew until I returned, she held a thread and refused to let it go.

I know she will be pleased, and she will be perplexed. I imagine her shrugging off compliments, with a certain giggle and a wave of her hand – ah go on! But we, we who know her value, we must drag her back up to her pedestal and bribe her up there with yellow rice and wine. We need her, her calm hand upon

the helm; her eyebrow raised. She is our fixed compass, our northern star.

She is my memory and my youth. She is one of the moments on which my life turned.

She is still that girl, the one who points and says, "Sit here."

(A prose version of this was published in the Irish Times)

Authors note: Ms Ferns is still that same kind spirit. If I could give advice to our young women, and our old ones too, I'd say - Whenever possible, be that girl, the one who points and says, "sit here." Make room at your table for your sisters, of all kinds, and lift them all up.

The Last Word

For Kim Crowell, October 19th 1983 - April 29th 2016. A lovely person, devoted mother and friend.

    Drink all the coffee
    eat all the cake
    Walk in the rainstorms
    dance as the sun rises
    talk to strangers
    tell them your stories
    (Eat all that cake, please.)
    Wear all the colours
    stand at the front in photos
    dye your hair or let it be grey
    Sing all the songs
    travel every boreen
    cry all the tears
    (Drink all that coffee, do!)
    Hug all the children
    Love all those loves
    for the day passes in seconds
    and the night falls too soon
    Leave no book unread
    Leave no heart untouched
    and fight that good fight
    until we meet again.

IV

Dreams of Reality: In your mind

This series was written to raise awareness about Alzheimer's as a family carer. I cared for my Dad for almost 10 years as he struggled with dementia. Being a family carer in any capacity is
daunting, caring for someone with Dementia has its own peculiar challenges.
We do it, because we love them but there is no aspect of it that is easy.
Each of these poems was written for specific purpose, to reflect the experiences of myself and others.
These poems are dedicated to Charles Byrne

The Alzheimer Series

Each poem addresses a different aspect of the loneliness, stress and grief of caring for someone with Dementia. And occasionally the humour and wry moments, as well as the love and satisfaction of knowing we did our best.

Poems:

Questions - The first struggle is with acceptance. How can you or they accept what is happening? The most heartbreaking thing to witness is their fear, and bewilderment, and it is echoed in our hearts by our own.

Preservation - The realization that the things you share, the memories, are slipping away from them. We become curators of their memories and associations.

You Have to Laugh - If you didn't laugh, you'd cry. The first time he truly had no idea who I was.

Red Tape - Family carers (in Ireland, but I am assured elsewhere too) are faced with impossible bureaucratic hurdles to get even the basics of home visits, or respite care, let alone nursing home places.

Side Effects - Honestly, they expect family carers to deal with things trained nurses and pharmacists would find difficult.

Positivity - One of the worst things is to be told you're not being positive, you're too negative, you shouldn't take personal offense, as you cling to the last shred of sanity.

Nights Out - People will not always understand. My husband and I were ghosted by an entire group of friends because we were "too moany" and didn't have weekends away and nights out any more. Real friends will turn up and make you dinner.

Manifesto - Those final weeks and days are the worst. We sat by his bed day and night, and somewhere inside I knew he was annoyed at us for doing so. I certainly came away determined to instill this message in my own kids.

After - When they are finally at rest, one of the common pieces of consolation offered by people is that you can just remember the good times. This is not possible when you have been brutalized by Dementia, by its cruelty and pain. But it will come, in its own time.

The First Year Without You - Every missed event, every birthday, every anniversary - even if they haven't been mentally aware of them for years - feels bleak.

In Absentia - How do we move on? How to find a way to mark their memory and make them part of our present?

Some of these are particularly true for carers of those with Dementia and Alzheimer's while others address universal grief.

Questions

Every morning starts with his voice -
  in childhood, a reassuring bellow
  now the alarm clock of my senses
  prompting anxious query, what
  does he need, where is he, when
  did it happen, how
  do we help?
  Why is this happening?
  Why is this happening to him?

Preservation

I wish we could preserve
   memories in amber
   or suspended like flowers in
   epoxy resin,
   make pendants of them,
   wear them like earrings,
   glaze them. Varnish them. Protect
   them from glare, the corrosive
   acids of time and aging, replace them
   whenever he mislays them.

You Have to Laugh

In Lockdown, I cut my father's hair
   him seated in the kitchen chair
   Like a pleased child, tries to tip me twice
   says over and over, "Isn't it nice!"
   He sidles up to his son-in-law
   who asks him, is anything wrong?
   He points to me, his own blood -
   "Has that lady worked here long?"

Red Tape

I sent in a form
   they sent me back three
   plus requests for additional
   information
   I sent in three forms plus extra
   as requested. I wait.
   They respond. One more form,
   a consultant's report, a bank account
   number, a solicitor's letter
   and the soul of my first born.
   Only one of these things is a joke.

I respond. In triplicate, with two reports
   and a begging letter. No joke. I beg.
   Again, I wait.
   Silence. They are psyching me out,
   We are gunslingers, engaged in a deadly hand
   of nursing home poker.

Finally they lay their cards on the table
   I realize,
   when they call my bluff, for a percentage
   of everything my parents worked for;
   their home, their savings and

their pension - all of which is
pathetically, heart-breakingly
modest - I realize
they hold all the cards and I fold.
I folded long ago.
I send in one last form of capitulation.
I wait.

They ask for clarification and a copy of the
CSAR report.

Side Effects

Including but not limited to
   dizziness, hypertension, cerebral
   infarction
   vomiting, hypertension, grand mal seizure
   mini stroke.
   And they're just the ones that passed inspection.
   Post Marketing side effects are now a thing
   in my world.
   They include psychiatric disorders
   suicidal ideation, cardiac congestion.
   I run out of comprehension on page two.
   I have to google Hepatobiliary.
   I know what pancreatitis is.
   And we risk all this in the hope
   that he might recognize his own face in the mirror

Positivity

I loved it the first time I read it
Never argue, only agree
I thought it was a panacea
restoring a degree
of peace and harmony

At 4 am when he moves every stitch
of my mother's clothing out
onto the floor, banging on the door
I begin to doubt whether
the author knew the score

After a run of broken sleep
when he insists I'm his cleaner
I could not be keener to try
not to roar and cry, but I confess
in reality, I'm a mess.

Nights Out

Friends don't understand
   where am I these days?
   Where's my head at -
   I am selfish, they hint
   to miss this event, that night out.

Nights out, I explain, are out for me
   unless one of them can parent sit?
   Meds at nine-thirty, bed whenever
   he stops rearranging
   furniture in the sitting room.

Then if you could clean up -
   you'll know what I mean
   when you see it - and stay up until
   you're sure he's asleep. Set the alarm,
   yes, the house alarm, he might wander.
   Then yes, I can be the one,
   in glad rags sipping rosé.

Manifesto

When it is my turn
   to lie in a bed and take
   gasping breaths
   I want you to know
   my manifesto for dying.

Do not haunt my bedside
   don't be a fixture on ward
   Visit the nursing home once a day
   Let the hospice be but a stop
   On your way home to food and company

If you are sitting by my bed
   and the sun shines, a pale gold over
   early spring flowers, get up
   Walk outside. Breathe fresh air, dance in
   the showers of soft rain
   Touch leaves and smell the blossoms

If your friend rings, take the call
   If your child is bored, take them away from
   this and push them on the swings in that
   park, the one with brightly painted railings.
   As I wait to depart, honour me

   by embracing every moment of life

Yes, you will feel pain
   But you will also feel the warm air. You will
   look upon the tiny beauties of the living
   and among such things
   you will find me.

After

When they leave us
   it's not that we forget
   the hard words and the endless nights
   the fights, the flights, the empty hours
   the cold memories live with us still.
   We do not become whole with the laying of wreaths -
   we are not glass, to be wiped clean.

When they leave us,
   it is rather that we remember
   the warmth of a smile, the salt of tears
   cups of tea and books, the pleasures shared
   the shorthand of our lives, the threads
   of love and plans and dreams.
   Not all at once are they seen, but in glimpses
   and we can hope to see them whole.

The First Year Without You

Each one of us hangs a bauble
   with our name, upon the tree -
   the task of hanging yours now falls to me.
   Your name is spoken often still
   and dear to all our hearts -
   but the sight of it today tore mine apart.
   We have a new tradition now
   no matter what we do -
   we do the things we always did, missing you.

In Absentia

How do we mark the day -
   now the ritual of cake and candle is
   overtaken by another, the bell, incense
   and eulogy of a cold church
   on a spring morning - how do we
   count the ninety third voyage,
   your passing through space now a
   matter of belief and dreams
   and all the tangible weight of you
   vanished, like words spoken into the wind?

How do we celebrate the presence
   when the absence is a stone, a stumble
   that bruises every time? We rearrange
   and redesign, colour over the dark shapes;
   the indent in pillows smoothed out
   and one less plate laid, one less portion
   measured, but still we trip up.
   And I stand undecided in the doorway
   wondering if you would know
   if we lit a candle, in a slice frosted with icing?

About the Author

Geraldine Moorkens Byrne is a poet from Dublin, Ireland. Her work has been published in a wide variety of print and media. Her poetry draws heavily from Irish poetic forms, Early Irish literature and mythology but embraces modern concerns and activism as well as the intensely personal. She has been published in a wide range of print, e-zine, and visual media some of which are listed below. Her short story *A Stranger Among Friends*, was shortlisted in the Cunningham Short Story Competition in 2020 and published in the anthology *Who Are We? (Willowdown Books 2020)*

Published works of poetry include:
  The Jane Raeburn Anthology
  Where The Hazel Falls
  Prairie Poetry
  Anthology of Small Things
  Of Gods and Radicals
  Asia Geographic
  Sixteen - The 1916 Commemorative Magazine
  The John Creedon/Listowel Writers Festival (RTE radio one)
  The American Dowsing Journal
  Poems from the Lockdown

and more.

She is also the author of several mystery novels, including The Caroline Jordan Mysteries, The Music Shop Mysteries and, under the pen name Nina Hayes, The Old Bat Chronicles. She has written several short stories including A Stranger Among Friends (The Cunningham Short Story Competition Winners Anthology, Willowbrook Books.) Requiem for a Violin (The Little Shop of Murders Anthology 2023)

Geraldine teaches classes on both Irish folk magic and Irish poetic forms with the Irish Pagan School. She lives in Dublin, with her family, and when not writing is the curator of a vast yarn collection. From 1992 - 2021 she ran the family music shop, the famous Charles Byrne Music in Stephen Street Lower.

She is the author of **Draíocht Ceoil, The Sound of Magic in Irish Traditions.**

You can buy her Mystery and Cozy Mystery books from BuyTheBook.ie (signed) order through your local bookshop or library, or online at Amazon, Barnes and Nobles and other retailers.

You can connect with me on:
- http://www.geraldinemoorkensbyrne.com
- https://www.twitter.com/gercelt
- https://www.faccbook.com/geraldinemoorkensbyrne
- https://irishpaganschool.com/courses/author/704627
- https://www.buythebook.ie/shop/geraldine-moorkens-byrne-author

Subscribe to my newsletter:
- https://mailchi.mp/a3703e884df5/author-sign-up

Also by Geraldine Moorkens Byrne

The Body Politic

When Minister Fitzpatrick is found dead at his desk Caroline Jordan loses her main client, plunging her tiny PR firm into chaos. A new VIP client could be their savior but with rumours flying about how the Justice Minister met his end, a strange cop dogging her footsteps, and ruthless killer stalking the corridors of power, can Caroline survive Irish Politics?

A fun murder mystery set at the heart of Dublin's social and political Elite.

The Body Count

Things are going well at Jordan PR. The beleaguered Bank of Leinster need a new PR team and this could be their biggest contract yet. But the discovery of a corpse in the bank's meeting room throws everything into disarray, and brings the Special Crimes Unit back into their lives. Caroline soon finds that the Bank holds old secrets, and someone is willing to kill for them. Can she solve the murder before the Body Count rises?

The Old Bat Chronicles

A magical mystery series set in Bramble Lane, in a leafy Dublin suburb. Eve Caulton finds a new home in Kimberly Cottage, aged fifty and freshly divorced. But when murder threatens her new life, her very special neighbour Dymphna and her band of Wise Women step up to help! Follow Eve and the Old Bats through a series of rollicking adventures filled with warmth, heart and a dollop of authentic Irish magic.

Written under the pen name Nina Hayes

www.ingramcontent.com/pod-product-compliance
Lightning Source LLC
Chambersburg PA
CBHW030553080526
44585CB00012B/363